> **Occupational Safety and Health Act of 1970**
> "To assure safe and healthful working conditions for working men and women; by authorizing enforcement of the standards developed under the Act; by assisting and encouraging the States in their efforts to assure safe and healthful working conditions; by providing for research, information, education, and training in the field of occupational safety and health."

Recommendations
for Workplace Violence
Prevention Programs

in Late-Night Retail Establishments

**Occupational Safety and Health Administration
U.S. Department of Labor**

OSHA 3153-12R
2009

These recommendations are advisory in nature and informational in content. It is not a standard or regulation, and it neither creates new legal obligations nor alters existing obligations created by OSHA standards or the *Occupational Safety and Health Act*. Pursuant to the OSH Act, employers must comply with safety and health standards and regulations issued and enforced either by OSHA or by an OSHA-approved State Plan. These "state plan states" may have standards that address workplace violence. Employers are responsible for following the standards in the states where they have worksites. Appendix C provides a summary of existing State Plan standards addressing workplace violence. In addition, the Act's General Duty Clause, Section 5(a)(1), requires employers to provide their employees with a workplace free from recognized hazards likely to cause death or serious physical harm.

Acknowledgements

Many people and organizations contributed to this publication. OSHA wishes to thank the contributing researchers, educators, representatives of victims' groups, industry, and law enforcement personnel for their comments and suggestions.

OSHA®
**Occupational Safety and
Health Administration**

Contents

Introduction

Workplace violence, whether it is defined narrowly to include only violent criminal acts, or broadly to include verbal threats, has long affected retail workers. OSHA developed these recommendations to help late-night retail employers design and implement prevention programs tailored to the workplace violence hazards in their businesses. Existing data, while limited, suggests that late-night retail establishments, such as convenience stores, liquor stores, and gasoline stations, experience relatively high homicide and assault rates. This booklet is meant to provide guidance to retail employers so they may avoid such incidents whenever possible. By recognizing the hazards that lead to violent incidents and implementing appropriate prevention and control measures, employers will improve the safety of their workers. OSHA encourages employers to establish violence prevention programs and to track their progress in reducing work-related assaults. Although not every incident can be prevented, the severity of injuries sustained by workers can be reduced. Adopting practical measures, such as those outlined in this publication, can significantly reduce this serious threat to worker safety.

Extent of the Problem

According to the Bureau of Labor Statistics' (BLS) *Census of Fatal Occupational Injuries* for 2007, assaults and violent acts claimed 864 lives in 2007 and represented over 15% of the total 5,657 workplace fatalities in the United States. Homicides represented the majority of these violent acts, claiming 628 lives in 2007, or 11% of fatalities. Over 26% of those homicides (a total of 167) occurred in the retail trades, with 39 occurring at convenience stores, 32 occurring at gasoline stations and 7 occurring at liquor stores. While homicides have shown a marked overall decline since 1994 when they peaked at 1,080, they were the third leading cause of work-related deaths in 2007, and remain a serious risk for late-night retail workers.

Data from the BLS Survey of *Occupational Injuries and Illnesses* for 2007 suggests that non-fatal violent incidents have also impacted retail work sites. Overall, private industry experienced a 2.6 incidence rate[1] for assault and violent acts (a total of 24,230 incidents) but convenience stores experienced a rate of over 20.0 (a total of 410 incidents). In 2005, BLS conducted another survey specifically

on workplace violence prevention.[2] In this survey, BLS asked employers about their establishments' operations, programs and policies regarding workplace violence. These survey results showed that while 4.8% of all private industry establishments reported experiencing some form of workplace violence, 7.1% of employers from the retail trade reported experiencing such an incident. Retail trade establishments which did experience such incidents also reported having higher rates of absenteeism due to these incidents than did all private industry establishments. Surprisingly, while 28.3% of retail trade employers reported that such incidents had negative impacts on workers, only 1.9% reported changing their program or policy after an incident occurred.

According to an earlier survey conducted by the U.S. Bureau of Justice Statistics (BJS), retail sales occupations had the third highest victimization rate, after workers in the law enforcement and mental health professions. The BJS National Crime Victimization Survey (1993-1999) found that 20 out of 1,000 workers in retail had experienced some form of simple or aggravated assault in the workplace annually, and the rate for convenience store and gas station workers was much higher. Their rate was 53.9 and 68.3 per 1,000 workers, respectively. In addition, 21% of all workplace robberies involved personnel in retail sales.

The risk factors

A number of factors put late-night retail workers at risk. These include:

- The exchange of money (making them targets for robbery);
- Solo work and isolated work sites;
- The sale of alcohol;
- Poorly lit stores and parking areas; and
- Lack of staff training in recognizing and managing escalating hostile and aggressive behavior.

An Effective Violence Prevention Program

In January 1989, OSHA published voluntary, generic safety and health program management guidelines,[3] followed by recommendations for work-

---

[1] Incidence rates for non-fatal injuries and illnesses involving days away from work is defined as the number of incidents per 10,000 full-time workers.

[2] BLS conducted this voluntary survey for the National Institute for Occupational Safety and Health and the Centers for Disease Control and Prevention. The *Survey of Workplace Violence Prevention* looked at the prevalence of security features, the risks facing workers, employer policies and training, and related topics associated with maintaining a safe work environment.

[3] OSHA's *Safety and Health Program Management Guidelines; Issuance of Voluntary Guidelines*, 54 Fed. Reg. 3904-3916, January 26, 1989.

OSHA®
Occupational Safety and
Health Administration

place violence prevention programs in late-night retail establishments, published in 1998.[4] The violence prevention information presented in this document builds on those guidelines by identifying risk factors and describing some feasible solutions. Although not exhaustive, these workplace violence guidelines include policy recommendations and practical corrective methods to help prevent and mitigate the effects of workplace violence in late-night retail establishments.

The goal of this document is to encourage employers to implement programs to identify the potential risks of workplace violence and to implement corrective measures. These recommendations are not a "model program" or a rigid package of violence prevention steps uniformly applicable to all establishments. No single strategy is appropriate for all businesses, since environmental and other risk factors for workplace violence differ widely among workplaces. Employers may use a combination of strategies recommended in this document, as appropriate, for their particular workplace.

While OSHA encourages employers to develop a written program for workplace violence prevention,

the extent to which the components of the program are in writing is less important than how effective the program is in practice. By implementing appropriate hazard prevention and control measures, and ensuring management and worker involvement, employers will take the most critical steps in protecting their workplace from violent acts. A written statement of policy serves as a touchstone for the many separate plans, procedures and actions required for an effective prevention program. In smaller establishments, a program can be effective without being documented. As the size of a workplace or the complexity of hazard control increases, written guidance becomes more important as a way to ensure clear communication and consistent application of policies and procedures. An employer could create a separate workplace violence prevention program or incorporate this information into an existing accident prevention program, employee handbook, or manual of standard operating procedures.

These recommendations are not a new standard or regulation and do not create any new OSHA duties. Therefore, these recommendations are not intended to establish a legal standard of care with respect to workplace violence. Accordingly, these recommendations do not impose any new legal obligations or constraints on employers or the states.

---

[4] OSHA's *Recommendations for Workplace Violence Prevention Programs in Late-Night Retail Establishments, OSHA Publication 3153, 1998.*

Violence Prevention Programs

Violence prevention programs should set clear goals and objectives to prevent workplace violence. The goals and objectives must be suitable for the size and complexity of workplace operations. In addition, the program should be adaptable to different situations at the worksite. Whatever format the program takes, it is critical that employers clearly explain the prevention program to all workers.

At a minimum, workplace violence prevention programs should:

- Establish a clear policy for workplace violence, verbal and nonverbal threats and related actions. All personnel employed in the retail establishment should know the policy.

- Ensure that no worker who reports or experiences workplace violence faces reprisals.[5]

- Encourage workers to promptly report incidents and suggest ways to reduce or eliminate risks. Require records of incidents to assess risk and measure progress.

- Outline a comprehensive plan for maintaining security in the workplace. The plan should include establishing a liaison with law enforcement representatives and others who can help identify ways to prevent and mitigate workplace violence.

- Assign responsibility and authority for the program to individuals or teams with appropriate training and skills. Ensure that adequate resources are available and that those responsible for the program develop expertise on workplace violence prevention in late-night retail settings.

- Affirm management commitment to an environment that places as much importance on worker safety and health as on serving store patrons.

Elements of an Effective Violence Prevention Program

The four components of an effective safety and health management system also apply to the prevention of workplace violence, and are:

- Management commitment and worker involvement;

- Worksite analysis;
- Hazard prevention and control; and
- Safety and health training.

Management Commitment and Worker Involvement

Management commitment and worker involvement are complementary and essential elements of an effective safety and health management system. To ensure an effective program, management and frontline workers must work together. If employers opt to use a team or committee approach to addressing this element they must be careful to comply with the applicable provisions of the *National Labor Relations Act*.[6]

Management Commitment

By obligating resources – both human capital and financial – management provides the motivation and ability to effectively address workplace violence. Management commitment should include:

- Demonstrating organizational concern for worker emotional and physical safety and health, which includes medical and psychological counseling and debriefing for personnel who experience or witness assaults and other violent incidents;

- Exhibiting equal commitment to the safety and health of workers and store patrons;

- Assigning responsibility for the various aspects of the workplace violence prevention program to ensure that all managers, supervisors and workers understand their obligations;

- Allocating appropriate authority and resources to all responsible parties;

- Maintaining a system of accountability for involved managers, supervisors and workers;

- Supporting and implementing appropriate recommendations from safety and health committees; and

- Working constructively with other parties, such as landlords, lessees, local police and other public safety agencies to improve security in and around the worksite.

Worker Involvement

Worker involvement in violence prevention is especially critical in the late-night retail setting.

---

[5] Section 11(c)(1) of the OSH Act applies to protected activity involving hazards of workplace violence as it does for other health and safety matters: "No person shall discharge or in any manner discriminate against any employee because such employee has filed any complaint or instituted or caused to be instituted any proceedings under or related to this Act or has testified or is about to testify in any such proceeding or because of the exercise by such employee on behalf of himself or others of any right afforded by this Act."

[6] 29 U.S.C. 158(a)(2) stipulates that an employer can ask that an employee confer but without loss of time or pay.

Occupational Safety and Health Administration

Frontline workers are often the most knowledgeable of business procedures and the business environment – especially in situations where no manager is on duty. Workers' experiences can help to identify practical solutions to safety challenges. The more inclusive the approach to developing a workplace violence prevention plan, the more comprehensive it will be. In addition, workers who are engaged in violence prevention programs are more likely to support them and ensure their effectiveness.

Workers should be involved by:
- Contributing to the development of procedures that address safety and security concerns, including responding to surveys on these issues;
- Understanding and complying with the workplace violence prevention program and safety and security measures;
- Reporting violent incidents promptly and accurately;
- Participating in safety and health committees or teams that receive reports of violent incidents or security problems, make facility inspections and respond with recommendations for corrective strategies; and
- Taking part in training programs and sharing on-the-job experiences that cover techniques to recognize escalating agitation, aggressive behavior or criminal intent.

Worksite Analysis

A worksite analysis involves a step-by-step assessment to identify environmental and operational risks for violence. The analysis entails reviewing specific procedures or operations that contribute to hazards, identifying areas where hazards may develop and performing periodic safety audits. Since the hazard analysis is the foundation for the violence prevention program, it is important for the employer to carefully consider the person(s) or team that will conduct the analysis. If a team is used, it should include representatives from senior management, operations, workers, security, occupational safety and health personnel, legal and human resources staff. A small business may only need to assign the duty to a single worker or consultant.

The recommended program for worksite analysis includes, but is not limited to:
- Analyzing and tracking records;
- Conducting screening surveys; and
- Analyzing workplace security.

Records Review and Analysis

To begin a hazard analysis an employer should review previous business experiences for at least two or three years. The employer should collect and examine any medical, safety, workers' compensation and insurance records to identify any incidents of workplace violence. The review should include the OSHA Log of Work-Related Injuries and Illnesses (OSHA Form 300), if the employer is required to maintain one.[7] In addition, worker and police reports of incidents or near-incidents of assaults or aggressive behavior should be examined to identify and analyze trends in assaults relative to particular:
- Job titles;
- Workstations; and
- Date and time of day.

Through this analysis, an employer can identify the frequency and severity of incidents to establish a baseline for measuring improvement. Employers with more than one store or worksite may review each location's history of violence. To learn about trends in the community or industry an employer may contact local businesses, trade associations, police departments and community and civic groups. An employer should use several years of data, if possible, to gain a clear understanding of the existing trends.

Conducting Screening Surveys

Finding few documented cases of workplace violence should not be dismissed as random, because incidents may go unreported or undocumented. Management may not be aware of low intensity incidents or threats of violence that workers experienced. A worker questionnaire or survey about workplace violence issues can identify:
- If customers have assaulted workers;
- If the business has had to address other crimes, such as shoplifting;
- If workers have been threatened or harassed while on duty;
- Whether firearms were carried and/or used;
- How many workers were on duty when incidents occurred;
- Whether police were called;

---

[7] 29 CFR Part 1904.1 exempts employers with 10 or fewer employees at all times during a calendar year from maintaining an OSHA injury and illness log. In addition, 29 CFR 1904.2 exempts businesses classified in specific low-hazard retail, service, finance, insurance, or real estate industry from keeping these injury and illness records.

- What workers were doing before and during the incident;
- Whether preventive measures were in place at the time of the incident and whether they were implemented;
- Where incidents occurred; and
- How often these incidents occurred.

Employers may also use surveys to solicit workers' ideas on the potential for violent incidents and to identify or confirm the need for improved security measures. Detailed baseline screening surveys can help pinpoint tasks that put workers at risk. Periodic surveys, conducted at least annually or when business operations change or workplace violence incidents occur, can help employers identify new or previously unnoticed risk factors in work practices, procedures or controls. After these reviews, employers should provide feedback and follow-up with their workers.

Employers may choose to use independent reviewers to conduct and analyze these surveys. Independent reviewers, such as safety and health professionals, law enforcement/security specialists and insurance safety auditors, may offer advice to strengthen programs. These experts can also provide fresh perspectives to improve a violence prevention program.

Workplace Security Analysis

Employers should have the designated team, worker or consultant periodically inspect the worksite and evaluate job tasks to identify hazards, conditions, operations and situations that could expose workers to violence. An initial walkthrough survey should be conducted to identify risks and establish a baseline. To find areas requiring further evaluation, the team or coordinator should:

- Analyze incidents, including the characteristics of assailants and victims. Incident descriptions should include an account of what happened before and during the incident, and the relevant details of the situation and its outcome. When possible, someone should obtain police reports and recommendations.

- Identify jobs or locations with the greatest risk of violence as well as processes and procedures that put workers at risk of assault. The analysis should include an estimate of the frequency and time when the risk of violence is greatest.

- Note high risk factors such as types of store patrons or environmental factors, such as: building layouts, interior and exterior lighting, com-

munication systems (such as telephones), and where security systems are installed.

- Evaluate the effectiveness of existing security measures, including engineering controls. Analysis should include whether or not security measures are being implemented and whether or not they reduce or eliminate risk factors. If security measures are not being implemented, the analysis should determine what has inhibited their use.

Appendix A contains some sample checklists that may assist employers in developing their own security analyses. Trade associations and other organizations may also have materials that can assist employers in assessing the risk of violent incidents at their worksites. In addition, some local law enforcement agencies provide free advice to business owners on ways to reduce exposure to crime. As with the workplace surveys, employers may choose to hire independent consultants to analyze their worksites for security weaknesses.

Hazard Prevention and Control

By effectively preventing and controlling workplace violence hazards, employers are better able to protect workers and avoid workplace incidents. After hazards are identified through the systematic worksite analysis, employers will need to take steps to prevent or control those hazards. Employers or someone they designate should develop measures that include engineering, procedural, and/or administrative changes to reduce or eliminate the likelihood of violent incidents. Employers will likely need to use a combination of controls to manage the hazards identified through their hazard analyses but should carefully assess the effectiveness of each type of approach. Engineering controls are considered the most effective because they make physical improvements without any dependence on human behavior. If a given situation does not allow for engineering controls, employers should next consider procedural and administrative changes. Once prevention and control measures are in place, employers should ensure that procedures are followed and that workers are supported.

Minimizing Risk through Engineering Controls and Workplace Adaptations

Engineering controls remove the hazard from the workplace or create a barrier between the worker and the hazard. Several measures, such as those described in the following paragraphs, can effectively prevent or control workplace hazards at retail

establishments. The selection of any measure should be based on the hazards identified in the workplace security analysis.

Given that late-night retail businesses are prone to robberies, employers should seek to reduce their risk by improving visibility and surveillance, controlling customers' access, and limiting the availability of cash. Such measures could include:

- Limiting window signs to low or high locations and keeping shelving low so that workers can see incoming customers and so that police can observe what is occurring from the outside of the store;
- Ensuring the customer service and cash register areas are visible from outside the establishment;
- Placing curved mirrors at hallway intersections or concealed areas;
- Maintaining adequate lighting inside and outside the establishment;
- Installing video surveillance equipment and closed circuit TV to increase the likelihood of identification of perpetrators;
- Using door detectors so that workers are alerted when someone enters the store;
- Having height markers on exit doors to help witnesses provide more accurate descriptions of assailants;
- Installing and regularly maintaining alarm systems and other security devices, panic buttons, handheld alarms or noise devices, cellular phones and private channel radios where risk is apparent or may be anticipated;
- Arranging for a reliable response system when an alarm is triggered;
- Installing fences and other structures to direct the flow of customer traffic into and around the store;
- Controlling access to the store with door entry (buzzer) systems;
- Installing physical barriers such as bullet-resistant enclosures with pass-through windows between customers and workers; and
- Using drop safes to limit the availability of cash to cashiers and posting signs which state that cashiers have limited access to cash.

Minimizing Risk through Administrative and Work Practice Controls

Administrative and work practice controls affect the way workers perform their jobs or specific tasks. Changes in work practices and administrative pro-

cedures can help prevent violent incidents. Often policies are needed to ensure that the engineering controls are implemented and used effectively. For example, employers should:

- Integrate violence prevention activities into daily procedures, such as checking lighting, locks, and security cameras to help maintain a secure worksite.
- Require workers to use the drop safes and keep a minimal amount of cash in each register.
- Develop and implement procedures for the correct use of physical barriers, such as enclosures and pass-through windows.
- Establish a policy of when doors should be locked. Require workers to keep doors locked before and after official business hours. Require workers to lock doors used for deliveries and garbage removal when not in use. In addition, require that deliveries be made during normal daytime operations.
- Develop and implement emergency procedures for workers to use in case of a robbery or security breach – such as calling the police or triggering an alarm.

Other administrative and work practice controls, independent of engineering controls include:

- Prohibit transactions with large bills (over $20). If this is not practical because of frequent transactions over $20, cash levels should be kept as low as practical. Workers should not carry business receipts on their persons unless it is absolutely necessary.
- When possible, increase staffing levels at stores with a history of robbery or assaults, or located in high crime areas. Use the "buddy system," especially when personal safety may be threatened.
- Establish rules and practices to ensure that workers can walk to garbage areas and outdoor storage areas without increasing their risk of assault.
- Establish liaison with local police and state prosecutors. Report all incidents of violence. Give police physical layouts of facilities to expedite investigations.
- Require workers to report all assaults or threats to a supervisor or manager (for example, through a confidential interview). Keep log books and reports of such incidents to help determine any necessary actions to prevent recurrences.

- Advise workers of company procedures for requesting police assistance or filing charges when assaulted if necessary.

- Provide management support during emergencies. Respond promptly to all complaints.

- Set up a trained response team to respond to emergencies.

- Use properly trained security officers to deal with aggressive behavior. Follow written security procedures.

- Discourage workers from wearing necklaces or chains to help prevent possible strangulation in confrontational situations.

- Provide staff members with security escorts to parking areas in evening or late hours. Ensure that parking areas are highly visible, well lit and safely accessible to the building.

Administrative controls work only if they are followed. Employers should monitor workers regularly to ensure that proper work practices are being used. Employers should also provide periodic constructive feedback to workers to ensure that they understand and appreciate the importance of these procedures.

Employer Responses to Incidents of Violence

Post-incident responses and evaluations are essential for an effective violence prevention program. Policies should include standard operating procedures for management and workers to follow in the aftermath of a violent incident. Response procedures should ensure that the incident is properly investigated, workers receive the appropriate attention and, in the event of injury, injured workers receive prompt and appropriate medical treatment. Such procedures may include the following:

- Providing prompt first aid and emergency medical treatment for injured workers, which may include transportation to the local emergency medical facility.

- Reporting incidents to the police or notifying other authorities as required by applicable laws and regulations.[8]

- Securing the premises to safeguard evidence and reduce distractions during the post-incident response process so that police or authorities may investigate properly.

- Preparing an incident report immediately after the incident, noting details that might be forgot-

ten over time. Appendix B contains sample incident report forms that an employer may use or adapt.

- Informing management about the incident.

Victims of workplace violence suffer a variety of consequences, in addition to their actual physical injuries. These may include:

- Short- and long-term psychological trauma;

- Fear of returning to work;

- Changes in relationships with coworkers and family;

- Feelings of incompetence, guilt, powerlessness; and

- Fear of criticism by supervisors or managers.

Consequently, a strong follow-up program for these workers will not only help them to deal with these problems, but also help prepare them to confront or prevent future incidents of violence.

Several types of assistance can be incorporated into the post-incident response. For example, trauma crisis counseling, critical incident stress debriefing or employee assistance programs may be provided to assist victims. Certified employee assistance professionals, psychologists, psychiatrists, clinical nurse specialists or social workers may provide this counseling or the employer may refer workers to an outside specialist. In addition, the employer may establish an employee counseling service, peer counseling or support groups.

Counselors should be well trained and have a good understanding of the issues and consequences of assaults and other aggressive, violent behavior. Appropriate and promptly rendered post-incident debriefings and counseling reduce acute psychological trauma and general stress levels among victims and witnesses. In addition, this type of counseling educates staff about workplace violence and positively influences workplace and organizational cultural norms to reduce trauma associated with future incidents.

Safety and Health Training

Training and education ensure that all staff members are aware of potential security hazards and how to protect themselves and their coworkers through established policies and procedures. Workers with different jobs and responsibilities may need different types and levels of training.

Training for All Employees

Every employee, including supervisors and managers, should understand the concept of "universal

---

[8] As required by 29 CFR 1904.39(a), all employers must report to OSHA, within eight hours, a fatality resulting from a workplace incident or the hospitalization of three or more employees resulting from a workplace incident.

precautions for violence,"[9] which refers to the concept that violence should be expected but can be avoided or mitigated through proper precautionary preparation. Workers need to know the specific hazards associated with their jobs and worksite to help them minimize their risk of assault and injury. Training should include information on worksite-specific potential hazards and instructions on how to control those hazards. Training should also include guidance to limit workers from intervening in workplace altercations whenever possible unless enough staff or emergency response teams and security personnel are available. Topics may include the following:

- An overview of the potential risk of assault;
- The workplace violence prevention policy;
- Operational procedures, such as cash handling rules, designed to reduce risk;
- Proper use of security measures and engineering controls designed to reduce risk;
- Early recognition of escalating behavior or recognition of warning signs of situations that may lead to assaults;
- Behavioral strategies such as conflict resolution and aggression management techniques to defuse tense situations and reduce the likelihood of a violent outcome;
- The location and operation of safety devices such as alarm systems, along with required maintenance schedules and procedures;
- Policies and procedures for reporting the incident to the proper authorities, as well as record-keeping;
- Policies and procedures for obtaining medical care, counseling, workers' compensation or legal assistance after a violent episode or injury;
- Specific instructions on how to respond to a robbery such as turning over money or valuables without resistance, and how to respond to attempted shoplifting; and
- Emergency action procedures to be followed in the event of a robbery or violent incident.

Qualified trainers should provide instruction at the comprehension level appropriate for workers. Effective training programs involve role-playing, simulations and drills. At a minimum, employers should provide required training annually. Workers

who forget safety measures should be retrained. New, reassigned, temporary and visiting workers should receive the same training as permanent staff. In addition, establishments with high worker turnover may need to provide training more frequently.

The training program should also include an evaluation. At least annually, the team or coordinator responsible for the program should review its content, methods and the frequency of training. Program evaluations may involve supervisor and worker interviews, testing, observing, and reviewing reports of behavior of individuals in threatening situations.

Training for Supervisors/Managers and Security Personnel

Supervisors and managers need to recognize high-risk situations, so they can ensure that workers are not placed in assignments that compromise their safety. Following training, supervisors and managers should be able to recognize a potentially hazardous situation and to make any necessary changes in the physical worksite and/or policies and procedures to reduce or eliminate hazards. They should also be able to handle traumatized workers.

Security personnel need specific training relating to the worksite, including the psychological components of handling aggressive and abusive store patrons, and ways to handle aggression and defuse hostile situations.

Recordkeeping and Program Evaluations

Recordkeeping and evaluations of the violence prevention program are necessary to determine its overall effectiveness and identify any deficiencies.

Records Employers Should Maintain

Recordkeeping is essential to the program's success. Good records help employers determine the severity of the problem, evaluate methods of hazard control and identify training needs. Records can be especially useful to large organizations and members of a business group or trade association who "pool" data. Through trend analysis, records of injuries, illnesses, accidents, assaults, hazards, corrective actions, histories and training can help identify problems and solutions for an effective program.

Employers can tailor their recordkeeping practices to the needs of their violence prevention program. Maintaining records enables employers to monitor ongoing efforts to deter workplace violence,

---

[9] The concept of "universal precautions" began in the medical field and refers to the practice of assuming that all patients are infectious and therefore requires avoiding contact with patients' bodily fluids by means of wearing the appropriate personal protective equipment.

to determine if a violence prevention program is working and to identify ways to improve it.

Important records employers may maintain include:

- OSHA Log of Work-Related Injuries and Illnesses (OSHA Form 300). Employers who are required to keep this log must record any new work-related injury that results in death, days away from work, days of restriction or job transfer, medical treatment beyond first aid, loss of consciousness or a significant injury diagnosed by a licensed healthcare professional. Injuries caused by assaults must be entered on the log if they meet the recording criteria.

- Medical reports of work injury and supervisors' reports for each recorded assault. These records should describe the type of assault, such as an unprovoked sudden attack or patron-to-patron altercation; who was assaulted; and all other circumstances of the incident. The records should include a description of the environment or location, potential or actual cost, lost work time that resulted and the nature of injuries sustained. These medical records are confidential documents and should be kept in a locked location under the direct responsibility of a healthcare professional.

- Records of incidents of abuse, verbal attacks or aggressive behavior that may be threatening, such as pushing or shouting and acts of aggression toward other clients. These records may be kept as part of an incident report. Employers should ensure that the affected department evaluates these records routinely. (See sample violence incident forms in Appendix B.)

- Documentation of minutes of safety meetings, records of hazard analyses and corrective actions recommended and taken.

- Records of all training programs, attendees and qualification of trainers.

Program Evaluation Elements
As part of their overall program, employers should evaluate their safety and security measures. Top management should review the program regularly, and with each incident, evaluate its success. Responsible parties (including managers, supervisors and workers) should reevaluate policies and procedures on a regular basis to identify deficiencies and take corrective action.

Management should share workplace violence prevention evaluation reports with all workers. Any changes in the programs should be discussed at regular meetings of the safety committee, and with union representatives or other worker groups.

All reports should protect worker confidentiality either by presenting only aggregate data or by removing personal identifiers if individual data are used.

The processes involved in an evaluation should include:

- Establishing a uniform violence reporting system and regular review of reports;

- Reviewing reports and minutes from staff meetings on safety and security issues;

- Analyzing trends and rates in injuries, illnesses or fatalities caused by violence relative to initial or "baseline" rates;

- Measuring improvement based on lowering the frequency and severity of workplace violence;

- Keeping up-to-date records of administrative and work practice changes to prevent workplace violence and to evaluate how well they work;

- Surveying workers before and after making job or worksite changes or installing security measures or new systems to determine their effectiveness;

- Keeping abreast of new strategies available to address violence in retail establishments, as they develop;

- Complying with OSHA and State requirements for recording and reporting injuries, illnesses and deaths; and

- Requesting periodic law enforcement or outside consultant review of the worksite for recommendations on improving worker safety.

OSHA
Occupational Safety and
Health Administration

Conclusion

Workplace violence has emerged as a major occupational safety and health issue in many industries, especially the retail trade. OSHA's voluntary recommendations offer systematic frameworks to help employers protect workers from risks of injury and death from occupationally-related violence. By treating workplace violence as a preventable hazard, employers can develop practical, effective strategies to protect their workers from this serious risk and provide a safe, healthful working environment.

Appendices

Appendix A:
Sample Workplace Violence Factors and Control Checklists

These sample checklists can help employers identify present or potential workplace violence problems. They contain various factors and controls that are commonly encountered in retail establishments.

Not all of the questions listed here fit all types of retail businesses, and these checklists obviously do not include all possible topics specific businesses need. Employers should expand, modify, and adapt these checklists to fit their own circumstances. These suggestions are not new regulations or standards, and the fact that an employer does not adopt a listed control does not prove a violation of the General Duty clause. ("N/A" stands for "not applicable").

Sample Checklist 1:

Yes	No	N/A	Environmental Factors
			Do workers exchange money with the public?
			Is the business open during evening or late-night hours?
			Is the site located in a high crime area?
			Has the site experienced a robbery in the past 3 years?
			Has the site experienced other violent acts in the past 3 years?
			Has the site experienced threats, harassment, or other abusive behavior in the past 3 years?
Yes	**No**	**N/A**	**Engineering Controls**
			Do workers have access to a telephone with an outside line?
			Are emergency telephone numbers for law enforcement, fire and medical services, and an internal contact person posted next to the phone?
			Are emergency telephone numbers programmed into company telephones?
			Is the entrance to the building easily seen from the street and free of heavy shrub growth?
			Is lighting bright in outside, parking and adjacent areas?
			Are windows and views outside and inside clear of advertising or other obstructions?
			Is the cash register in plain view of customers and police cruisers to deter robberies?
			Is there a working drop safe or time access safe to minimize cash on hand?
			Are security cameras and mirrors placed in locations that would deter robbers or provide greater security for employees?
			Are there height markers on exit doors to help witnesses provide more complete descriptions of assailants?
			Are employees protected through the use of bullet-resistant enclosures in locations with a history of robberies or assaults in a high crime area?
Yes	**No**	**N/A**	**Administrative/Work Practice Controls**
			Are there emergency procedures in place to address robberies and other acts of potential violence?
			Have workers been instructed to report suspicious persons or activities?
			Are workers trained in emergency response procedures for robberies and other crimes that may occur on the premises?

Yes	No	N/A	Administrative/Work Practice Controls (*continued*)
			Are workers trained in conflict resolution and in nonviolent response to threatening situations?
			Is cash control a key element of the establishment's violence and robbery prevention program?
			Does the site have a policy limiting the number of cash registers open during late-night hours?
			Does the site have a policy to maintain less than $50 in the cash register? (This may not be possible in stores that have lottery tickets and payouts.)
			Are signs posted notifying the public that limited cash, no drugs, and no other valuables are kept on the premises?
			Do workers have at least one other person throughout their shifts, or are other protective measures utilized when workers are working alone in locations with a history of robberies or assaults in a high crime area?
			Are there procedures in place to assure the safety of workers who open and close the store?

Sample Checklist 2 – Self Inspection Security Checklist:

Reprinted with permission of the Hartford Financial Services Group, Inc., *Workplace Violence Prevention Program Loss Control TIPS* – Technical Information Paper Series

Facility: _____

Inspector: _____

Date of Inspection: _____

Security Control Plan?	☐ Yes	☐ No
If yes, does it contain:		
Policy Statement?	☐ Yes	☐ No
Review of Worker Incident Exposure?	☐ Yes	☐ No
Methods of Control?	☐ Yes	☐ No
If yes, does it include:		
Engineering	☐ Yes	☐ No
Work practice	☐ Yes	☐ No
Training	☐ Yes	☐ No
Reporting procedures	☐ Yes	☐ No
Recordkeeping	☐ Yes	☐ No
Counseling	☐ Yes	☐ No
Evaluation of incidents?	☐ Yes	☐ No
Floor Plan?	☐ Yes	☐ No
Protection of Assets?	☐ Yes	☐ No
Computer Security?	☐ Yes	☐ No
Plan accessible to all workers?	☐ Yes	☐ No
Plan reviewed and updated annually?	☐ Yes	☐ No
Plan reviewed and updated when tasks added or changed?	☐ Yes	☐ No
Policy statement by employer?	☐ Yes	☐ No
Work areas evaluated by employer?	☐ Yes	☐ No
If yes, how often? _____		
Engineering controls?	☐ Yes	☐ No
If yes, does it include:		
Mirrors to see around corners and in blind spots?	☐ Yes	☐ No
Landscaping to provide unobstructed view of the workplace?	☐ Yes	☐ No
"Fishbowl effect" to allow unobstructed view of the interior?	☐ Yes	☐ No
Limiting the posting of sale signs on windows?	☐ Yes	☐ No
Adequate lighting in and around the workplace?	☐ Yes	☐ No
Parking lot well lighted?	☐ Yes	☐ No
Door control(s)?	☐ Yes	☐ No
Panic button(s)?	☐ Yes	☐ No
Door detector(s)?	☐ Yes	☐ No
Closed circuit TV?	☐ Yes	☐ No

1 6

**Occupational Safety and
Health Administration**

Stationary metal detector? □ Yes □ No
Sound detection? □ Yes □ No
Intrusion detection system? □ Yes □ No
Intrusion panel? □ Yes □ No
Monitor(s)? □ Yes □ No
Videotape recorder? □ Yes □ No
Switcher? □ Yes □ No
Handheld metal detector? □ Yes □ No
Handheld video camera? □ Yes □ No
Personnel traps ("Sally Traps")? □ Yes □ No
Other? □ Yes □ No

Structural modifications
Plexiglas, glass guard, wire glass, partitions, etc.? □ **Yes** □ **No**

If yes, comment: _____

Security guards? □ **Yes** □ **No**
If yes, are there an appropriate number for the site? □ Yes □ No
Are they knowledgeable of the company WPVP Policy? □ Yes □ No
Indicate if they are:
_____ Contract Guards (1)
_____ In-house Workers (2)
At Entrance(s)? □ Yes □ No
Building Patrol? □ Yes □ No
Guards provided with communication? □ Yes □ No

*If yes, indicate what type:*_____

Guards receive training on Workplace Violence situations? □ Yes □ No

Comments: _____
_____

Work practice controls? □ **Yes** □ **No**
If yes, indicate:
Desks clear of objects which may become missiles? □ Yes □ No
Unobstructed office exits? □ Yes □ No
Vacant (Bare) cubicles available? □ Yes □ No
Reception area available? □ Yes □ No
Visitor/client sign in/out? □ Yes □ No
Visitor(s)/client(s) escorted? □ Yes □ No
One entrance used? □ Yes □ No
Separate interview area(s)? □ Yes □ No

I.D. badges used?	☐ Yes	☐ No
Emergency numbers posted by phones?	☐ Yes	☐ No
Internal phone system?	☐ Yes	☐ No

If yes, indicate:

Does it use 120 VAC building lines?	☐ Yes	☐ No
Does it use phone lines?	☐ Yes	☐ No
Internal procedures for conflict (problem) situations?	☐ Yes	☐ No
Procedures for worker dismissal?	☐ Yes	☐ No
Limit spouse & family visits to designated areas?	☐ Yes	☐ No
Key control procedures?	☐ Yes	☐ No
Access control to the workplace?	☐ Yes	☐ No
Objects which may become missiles removed from area?	☐ Yes	☐ No
Parking prohibited in fire zones?	☐ Yes	☐ No

Other:_____

_____

Workplace Violence Prevention Program © 2008 The Hartford Loss Control Department

**Occupational Safety and
Health Administration**

Sample Checklist 3 – Workplace Violence Inspection Checklist:
This checklist was adapted from *Violence on the Job: A Guidebook for Labor and Management*, published by the Labor Occupational Health Program, University of California, Berkeley.

Staffing

Is there someone responsible for building security?
☐ Yes   ☐ No   ☐ Sometimes   Notes _____
Who is it? _____

Are workers told who is responsible for security?
☐ Yes   ☐ No   ☐ Sometimes   Notes _____

Is adequate and trained staffing available to protect workers against assaults or other violence?
☐ Yes   ☐ No   ☐ Sometimes   Notes _____

Is there a "buddy system" to use when workers are in potentially dangerous situations?
☐ Yes   ☐ No   ☐ Sometimes   Notes _____

Are there trained security personnel accessible to workers in a timely manner?
☐ Yes   ☐ No   ☐ Sometimes   Notes _____

Do security personnel have sufficient authority to take all necessary action to ensure worker safety?
☐ Yes   ☐ No   ☐ Sometimes   Notes _____

Are security personnel provided outside the building?
☐ Yes   ☐ No   ☐ Sometimes   Notes _____

Is the parking lot attended or otherwise secure?
☐ Yes   ☐ No   ☐ Sometimes   Notes _____

Are security escorts available to walk workers to and from the parking lot?
☐ Yes   ☐ No   ☐ Sometimes   Notes _____

Training

Are workers trained in the emergency response plan (for example, escape routes, notifying the proper authorities)?
☐ Yes   ☐ No   ☐ Sometimes   Notes _____

Are workers trained to report violent incidents or threats?
☐ Yes   ☐ No   ☐ Sometimes   Notes _____

Are workers trained in how to handle difficult customers?
☐ Yes   ☐ No   ☐ Sometimes   Notes _____

Are workers trained in ways to prevent or defuse potentially violent situations?

☐ Yes ☐ No ☐ Sometimes Notes _____

Are workers trained in personal safety and self-defense?

☐ Yes ☐ No ☐ Sometimes Notes _____

Facility Design

Are there enough exits and adequate routes of escape?

☐ Yes ☐ No ☐ Sometimes Notes _____

Can exit doors be opened only from the inside to prevent unauthorized entry?

☐ Yes ☐ No ☐ Sometimes Notes _____

Is the lighting adequate to see clearly in indoor areas?

☐ Yes ☐ No ☐ Sometimes Notes _____

Are there worker-only work areas that are separate from public areas?

☐ Yes ☐ No ☐ Sometimes Notes _____

Is a secure place available for workers to store their personal belongings?

☐ Yes ☐ No ☐ Sometimes Notes _____

Are private, locked restrooms available for staff?

☐ Yes ☐ No ☐ Sometimes Notes _____

Security Measures

Does the workplace have:

Physical barriers (Plexiglas partitions, elevated counters to prevent people from jumping over them, bulletproof customer windows, etc.)?

☐ Yes ☐ No ☐ Sometimes Notes _____

Security cameras or closed-circuit TV in high risk areas?

☐ Yes ☐ No ☐ Sometimes Notes _____

Panic buttons (portable or fixed)?

☐ Yes ☐ No ☐ Sometimes Notes _____

Alarm systems?

☐ Yes ☐ No ☐ Sometimes Notes _____

Internal phone system to activate emergency assistance?

☐ Yes ☐ No ☐ Sometimes Notes _____

Phones with an outside line programmed to call 911?

☐ Yes ☐ No ☐ Sometimes Notes _____

Occupational Safety and Health Administration

Two-way radios, pagers or cellular phones?
☐ Yes ☐ No ☐ Sometimes Notes _____

Security mirrors (convex mirrors)?
☐ Yes ☐ No ☐ Sometimes Notes _____

Secured entry (buzzers)?
☐ Yes ☐ No ☐ Sometimes Notes _____

Personal alarm devices?
☐ Yes ☐ No ☐ Sometimes Notes _____

Outside The Facility

Do workers feel safe walking to and from the workplace?
☐ Yes ☐ No ☐ Sometimes Notes _____

Are the entrances to the building clearly visible from the street?
☐ Yes ☐ No ☐ Sometimes Notes _____

Is the area surrounding the building free of bushes or other hiding places?
☐ Yes ☐ No ☐ Sometimes Notes _____

Is video surveillance provided outside the building?
☐ Yes ☐ No ☐ Sometimes Notes _____

Is there enough lighting to see clearly outside the building?
☐ Yes ☐ No ☐ Sometimes Notes _____

Are all exterior walkways visible to security personnel?
☐ Yes ☐ No ☐ Sometimes Notes _____

Is there a nearby parking lot reserved for workers only?
☐ Yes ☐ No ☐ Sometimes Notes _____

Is the parking lot free of bushes or other hiding places?
☐ Yes ☐ No ☐ Sometimes Notes _____

Is there enough lighting to see clearly in the parking lot and when walking to the building?
☐ Yes ☐ No ☐ Sometimes Notes _____

Have neighboring facilities and businesses experienced violence or crime?
☐ Yes ☐ No ☐ Sometimes Notes _____

Workplace Procedures

Is public access to the building controlled?

☐ Yes   ☐ No   ☐ Sometimes   Notes _____

Are floor plans posted showing building entrances, exits?

☐ Yes   ☐ No   ☐ Sometimes   Notes _____

Are these floor plans visible only to staff and not to outsiders?

☐ Yes   ☐ No   ☐ Sometimes   Notes _____

Is other emergency information posted, such as telephone numbers?

☐ Yes   ☐ No   ☐ Sometimes   Notes _____

Are special security measures taken to protect people who work late at night (escorts, locked entrances, etc.)?

☐ Yes   ☐ No   ☐ Sometimes   Notes _____

Are authorized visitors to the building required to wear ID badges?

☐ Yes   ☐ No   ☐ Sometimes   Notes _____

Are identification tags required for staff (omitting personal information such as the person's last name and Social Security number)?

☐ Yes   ☐ No   ☐ Sometimes   Notes _____

Are workers notified of past violent activity?

☐ Yes   ☐ No   ☐ Sometimes   Notes _____

Is there an established liaison with local police?

☐ Yes   ☐ No   ☐ Sometimes   Notes _____

Are broken windows and locks repaired promptly?

☐ Yes   ☐ No   ☐ Sometimes   Notes _____

Are security devices (locks, cameras, alarms, etc.) tested on a regular basis and repaired promptly when necessary?

☐ Yes   ☐ No   ☐ Sometimes   Notes _____

Field Work

Staffing:

Is there adequate staffing in the establishment?

☐ Yes   ☐ No   ☐ Sometimes   Notes _____

Are escorts or "buddies" provided for people who work in potentially dangerous situations?

☐ Yes   ☐ No   ☐ Sometimes   Notes _____

Training:

Are workers briefed about the area in which they will be working (gang colors, neighborhood culture, language, drug activity, etc.)?

❑ Yes　　❑ No　　❑ Sometimes　　Notes _____

Are workers who work late at night or early mornings advised about special precautions to take?

❑ Yes　　❑ No　　❑ Sometimes　　Notes _____

Work Environment:

Is there enough lighting to see clearly in all areas where workers must go?

❑ Yes　　❑ No　　❑ Sometimes　　Notes _____

Are there safe places for workers to eat, use the restroom, store valuables, etc.?

❑ Yes　　❑ No　　❑ Sometimes　　Notes _____

Are there places where workers can go for protection in an emergency?

❑ Yes　　❑ No　　❑ Sometimes　　Notes _____

Is safe parking readily available for workers?

❑ Yes　　❑ No　　❑ Sometimes　　Notes _____

Security Measures:

Are workers provided two-way radios, pagers or cellular phones?

❑ Yes　　❑ No　　❑ Sometimes　　Notes _____

Are workers provided with personal alarm devices or portable panic buttons?

❑ Yes　　❑ No　　❑ Sometimes　　Notes _____

Are vehicle door and window locks controlled by the driver?

❑ Yes　　❑ No　　❑ Sometimes　　Notes _____

Are vehicles equipped with physical barriers (Plexiglas partitions, etc.)?

❑ Yes　　❑ No　　❑ Sometimes　　Notes _____

Work Procedures:

Are workers given maps and good directions covering the areas where they will be working?

❑ Yes　　❑ No　　❑ Sometimes　　Notes _____

Are workers given alternative routes to use in neighborhoods with a high crime rate?

❑ Yes　　❑ No　　❑ Sometimes　　Notes _____

Does a policy exist to allow workers to refuse service to unruly customers?

❑ Yes　　❑ No　　❑ Sometimes　　Notes _____

Has a liaison with the police been established?

❑ Yes ❑ No ❑ Sometimes Notes _____

Do workers avoid carrying unnecessary items, which someone could use as a weapon against them?

❑ Yes ❑ No ❑ Sometimes Notes _____

Is a safe vehicle or other transportation provided by the employer for use when conducting company business?

❑ Yes ❑ No ❑ Sometimes Notes _____

Are vehicles used in the field routinely inspected and kept in good working order?

❑ Yes ❑ No ❑ Sometimes Notes _____

Is there always someone who knows where each worker is while traveling during business hours?

❑ Yes ❑ No ❑ Sometimes Notes _____

Are workers notified of past violent acts committed by customers or other personnel?

❑ Yes ❑ No ❑ Sometimes Notes _____

Are special precautions taken when workers:

Perform "enforcement" functions (parking control officers, inspectors, etc.)?

❑ Yes ❑ No ❑ Sometimes Notes _____

Have to take something away from customers (illegal credit cards)?

❑ Yes ❑ No ❑ Sometimes Notes _____

Have contact with people who behave violently?

❑ Yes ❑ No ❑ Sometimes Notes _____

Have contact with dangerous animals (dogs, rodents, etc.)?

❑ Yes ❑ No ❑ Sometimes Notes _____

Sample Incident Report Form 1:
This incident report was adapted from *Violence on the Job: a Guidebook for Labor and Management*, published by the Labor Occupational Health Program, University of California, Berkeley.

Workplace Violence Incident Report Form

Personal Information

Name (*optional*)_____

☐ Male   ☐ Female

Job title _____

Facility/employer address

_____
_____
_____
_____

Years in current job _____

Incident Description

Date incident occurred _____

Time incident occurred _____

Location where incident occurred (*be specific*)

_____
_____
_____
_____
_____

Describe the incident

_____
_____
_____
_____
_____
_____

Type of incident (*check all that apply*)

☐ Grabbed	☐ Pushed	☐ Slapped
☐ Kicked	☐ Scratched	☐ Hit with fist
☐ Hit with object	☐ Bitten	☐ Knifed (or attempted)
☐ Shot (or attempted)	☐ Sexually assaulted	☐ Assaulted with weapon
☐ Threatened with weapon	☐ Verbally harassed	☐ Verbally threatened
☐ Bomb threat	☐ Animal attack	☐ Robbery
☐ Vandalism (employer's property)	☐ Vandalism (own property)	☐ Other
☐ Arson		

What type of weapon was used? How was the weapon obtained?

_____

_____

_____

_____

_____

Were you working alone? If no, who was with you that may have witnessed the incident?

_____

_____

_____

_____

_____

Were security personnel on duty at the time of the assault? If yes, was security notified? Did security respond? When?

_____

_____

_____

_____

_____

_____

Who threatened or assaulted you?

☐ Client/customer	☐ Patient	☐ Parent
☐ Student	☐ Family/friend of client or patient	
☐ Co-worker	☐ Supervisor/manager	☐ Stranger
☐ Passenger	☐ Person in custody	☐ Animal
☐ Spouse or partner	☐ Former spouse or partner	☐ Other
☐ Robber/burglar		

Were any threats made before the incident occurred? If yes, did you ever report to your supervisor or manager that you were threatened, harassed or suspicious that the attacker may become violent?

_____
_____
_____
_____

Incident Analysis

☐ Yes ☐ No   Has this type of incident occurred before at the workplace?

What do you think were the main factors that contributed to the incident?

_____
_____
_____
_____

What could have prevented or at least minimized the damage caused by this incident?

_____
_____
_____
_____

Post-Incident Response

☐ Yes ☐ No   Did you require medical attention as a result of the incident?

☐ Yes ☐ No   Did you miss work as a result of the incident?

☐ Yes ☐ No   Did you apply for workers' compensation?

☐ Yes ☐ No   Was the incident reported to a supervisor or manager?

☐ Yes ☐ No   Was a police report filed?

☐ Yes ☐ No   Was immediate counseling provided to affected workers and witnesses who desired it?

☐ Yes ☐ No   Was critical incident debriefing provided to all affected staff who desired it?

☐ Yes ☐ No   Was post-trauma (follow-up) counseling provided to all affected staff who desired it?

☐ Yes ☐ No   Was all counseling provided by a professional counselor?

☐ Yes ☐ No   Was the counseling effective?

☐ Yes ☐ No   Was the victim advised about legal rights?

Report completed by _____

Department/Job Title/Union Position_____

_____

Date _____ Phone number _____

E-mail _____

Sample Incident Report Form 2:

Reprinted with permission of the Hartford Financial Services Group, Inc., *Workplace Violence Prevention Program Loss Control TIPS—Technical Information Paper Series.*

Victim's Name _____ Job Title _____

Victim's Address _____

Home Phone Number _____ Work Phone Number _____

Employer's Name and Address _____

Department/Section _____

Victim's Social Security Number _____

Incident Date _____

Incident Time _____

Incident Location _____

Work Location (*if different*) _____

Type of Incident: (*check one*) ☐ Assault ☐ Robbery ☐ Harassment ☐ Disorderly Conduct
☐ Sex Offense ☐ Other (*Please Specify*) _____

(*See* **Definition of Incidents Worksheet**)

Were You Injured? ☐ Yes ☐ No

If yes, please specify your injuries and the location of any treatment

_____

_____

_____

_____

Did Police Respond to Incident ☐ Yes ☐ No

What Police Department _____

Police Report Filed ☐ Yes ☐ No

Report Number _____

Was Your Supervisor Notified ☐ Yes ☐ No

Supervisor's Name _____

Was the Local Union/Employee Representative Notified ☐ Yes ☐ No

Who should be notified _____

Was Any Action Taken By Employer (specify) _____

_____

Assailant/Perpetrator (*check one*) ☐ Intruder ☐ Customer ☐ Patient ☐ Resident
☐ Client ☐ Visitor ☐ Student ☐ Co-Worker ☐ Former Worker ☐ Supervisor
☐ Family/Friend ☐ Other (*specify*)

_____

21. Assailant/Perpetrator—Name/Address/Age (if known): _____

_____

_____

**Occupational Safety and
Health Administration**

Please Briefly Describe the Incident _____

_____

_____

Incident Disposition ☐ No action taken ☐ Arrest ☐ Warning ☐ Suspension
☐ Reprimand ☐ Other (*Please Specify*) _____

_____

Did The Incident Involve A Weapon: ☐ Yes   ☐ No
    Specify_____

Did You Lose Any Workdays: ☐ Yes   ☐ No
    Specify_____

Were You Singled Out Or Was The Violence Directed At More Than One Individual _____

_____

Were You Alone When The Incident Occurred_____

_____

Did You Have Any Reason To Believe Than An Incident
    Might Occur   ☐ Yes   ☐ No
    Why _____

Has This Type Or Similar Incident(s) Happened To You Or Your
    Co-workers: ☐ Yes   ☐ No
    Specify_____

Have You Had Any Counseling Or Support Since The Incident: ☐ Yes   ☐ No
    Specify_____

What Do You Feel Can Be Done In The Future To Avoid Such An Incident _____

_____

Was This Assailant Involved In Previous Incidents _____

_____

Are There Any Measures In Place To Prevent Similar Incidents: ☐ Yes   ☐ No
    Specify_____

Has Corrective Action Been Taken: ☐ Yes   ☐ No
    Specify_____

_____

_____

Comments _____

_____

_____

_____

_____

Definition of Incidents

Assault

The intentional use of physical injury, (impairment of physical condition or substantial pain) to another person, with or without a weapon or dangerous instrument.

Criminal Mischief

Intentional or reckless damaging of the property of another person without permission.

Disorderly Conduct

Intentionally causing public inconvenience, annoyance or alarm or recklessly creating a risk thereof by fighting (without injury) or violent, numinous (mysterious) or threatening behavior or making unreasonable noise, shouting abuse, misbehaving, disturbing an assembly or meeting or persons or creating hazardous conditions by an act which serves no legitimate purpose.

Harassment

Intentionally striking, shoving or kicking another or subjecting another person to physical contact, or threatening to do the same (without physical injury). ALSO, using abusive or obscene language or following a person in/about a public place, or engaging in a course of conduct which alarms or seriously annoys another person.

Larceny

Wrongful taking, depriving or withholding property from another (no force involved). Victim may or may not be present.

Menacing

Intentionally places or attempts to place another person in fear of imminent serious physical injury.

Reckless Endangerment

Subjecting individuals to danger by recklessly engaging in conduct which creates substantial risk of serious physical injury.

Robbery

Forcible stealing of another's property by use of threat or immediate physical force. Victim is present and aware of theft.

Sex Offense

Public Lewdness:	Exposure of sexual organs to others.
Sexual Abuse:	Subjecting another to sexual contact without consent.
Sodomy:	A deviant sexual act committed as in rape.
Rape:	Sexual intercourse without consent.

Workplace Violence Prevention Program © 2008 The Hartford Loss Control Department

OSHA
Occupational Safety and
Health Administration

Appendix C:
States with Workplace Violence Standards

Below are examples of State Plan standards that address workplace violence. If employers maintain businesses in any state plan states they should contact the state occupational safety and health office to ensure that they have the most current standards.

New Mexico

The New Mexico Environmental Improvement Board, which issues occupational safety and health standards, issued a regulation (11.5.6) that requires convenience stores open between the hours of 11 p.m. and 5 a.m. either to have two workers on duty, or one clerk and a security guard, or to install bulletproof glass or other safety features to limit access to store personnel. See www.nmenv.state.nm.us/NMED_regs/osha/11nmac5_6.doc for more information.

Washington

Several existing provisions of the Washington Administrative Code (WAC) may apply to the hazards of violence in the workplace. The provision that is specific to late-night retail is: WAC 296-832, the "Late Night Retail Workers Crime Protection Standard," provides specific violence-related direction to retail businesses that operate between 11:00 p.m. and 6:00 a.m. Restaurants, hotels, taverns and lodging facilities are beyond the scope of this rule. See http://lni.wa.gov/Safety/Rules/Policies/PDFs/WRD505.pdf for more information.

Appendix D:
Bibliography and References

Bibliography

Albence, M.T. (1994). "Convenient Targets: An Examination of Convenience Store Robberies in Carbondale, Illinois, from 1986 to 1993." *Unpublished Master's Thesis,* Southern Illinois University at Carbondale.

Alexander, R.H., Franklin, G.M., and Wolf, M.L. (1994). "The sexual assault of women at work in Washington State, 1980-1989." *American Journal of Public Health* 84 (4):640-642.

Amandus, H.E. (1995). "Reevaluation of the effectiveness of environmental designs to reduce robbery risk in Florida convenience stores." *Journal of Occupational and Environmental Medicine* 37:711-717.

Amandus, H.E. (1995). "Status of NIOSH research on prevention of robbery-related intentional injuries to convenience store workers." *National Institute of Justice Research Report: Trends, Risks, and Interventions in Lethal Violence, Proceedings of Third Annual Spring Symposium of the Homicide Research Working Group,* Atlanta, GA. pp. 217-228.

Amandus, H.E. (1997). "Convenience store robberies in selected metropolitan areas: Risk factors for employees injury." *Journal of Occupational and Environmental Medicine* 39(5): 442-447.

American Insurance Services Group, Inc. (1994). "Workplace Violence: A Prevention Program." New York, NY: American Insurance Services Group, Inc.

ASIS International (2005). *Workplace Violence Prevention and Response Guide.* (http://www.asisonline.org/guidelines/guidelineswpvfinal.pdf).

Askari, E. (1997). "Violence on the Job: A Guidebook for Labor and Management." Berkeley, CA: University of California.

Athena Research Corporation. (1981). "Robber Interview Report." Presented to Crime Committee of the Southland Corporation, Dallas, TX.

Bachman, R. (1994). "Violence and Theft in the Workplace." *National Crime Victimization Survey.* Washington, DC: U.S. Department of Justice, Bureau of Justice Statistics.

Bellamy, L. (1995). "Situational Crime Prevention Strategies for Combating Convenience Store Robbery." Unpublished paper, Rutgers, The State University of New Jersey.

Bellamy, L. (1996). "Situational Crime Prevention and Convenience Stores Robbery." *Security Journal* 7:41-52.

Calder, J.D. and Bauer, J.R. (1992). "Convenience Store Robberies: Security Measures and Store Robbery Incidents." *Journal of Criminal Justice* 20:553-556.

California State Department of Industrial Relations. (1994). *CAL/OSHA Guidelines for Workplace Security.* San Francisco, CA: Division of Occupational Safety and Health.

California State Department of Industrial Relations. (1995). *Model Injury and Illness Prevention Program for Workplace Security.*

Clarke, R.V. (1983) "Situational Crime Prevention: Its theoretical basis and practical scope." *Crime and Justice: An Annual Review of Research* 4:225-256.

Clifton, W., Jr. and Callahan, P.T. (1987) Convenience Store Robberies: An Intervention Strategy by the City of Gainesville; Gainesville, FL: Gainesville Police Department.

Convenience Business Security Act. (1992) Supplement to Florida Statutes 1991. (§§ 812.1701 — 812.1750).

Cook, P.J. (1987). "Robbery Violence." *Journal of Criminal Law & Criminology* 78(2) pp. 357-375.

Crow, W.J. and Bull, J.L. (1975). *Robbery Deterrence: An Applied Behavioral Science Demonstration.* La Jolla, CA: Western Behavioral Sciences Institute.

Crow, W.J., Erickson. R.J., and Scott, L. (1987), "Set Your Sights on Preventing Retail Violence." *Security Management* 31 (9): 60-64.

OSHA
Occupational Safety and
Health Administration

Degner, R.L. et al. (1983), "Food Store Robberies in Florida: Detailed Crime Statistics." Florida Agricultural Market Research Center, Gainesville, FL.

Erickson, R.J. (1991). "Convenience Store Homicide and Rape." In National Association of Convenience Stores (Ed.). *Convenience Store Security*. Alexandria, VA. pp. 29-101.

Erickson, R.J. (1995). "Employer Liability for Workplace Violence." In Fitzpatrick, R. *Tips on Employment Law* 5:1-7. Washington, DC, American Bar Association.

Erickson, R.J. (1996). *Armed Robbers and Their Crimes*. Seattle, WA: Athena Research.

Erickson, R.J. (1996) "Retail Employees as a Group at Risk for Violence." *Occupational Medicines: State of the Art Reviews* 11(2): 269-275.

Erickson, R.J. (1998). *Convenience Store Security at the Millennium*. Alexandria, VA: National Association of Convenience Stores.

Federal Bureau of Investigation (1993). Crimes in the United States: Uniform Crime Reports. Washington, DC: United States Department of Justice.

Figlio, R. and Aurand, S. (1991). "An Assessment of Robbery Deterrence Measures at Convenience Stores." In National Association of Convenience Stores (Ed.). *Convenience Store Security* 103-138. Alexandria, VA. pp. 103-138.

Flannery, R.B., et al. (1991). "A program to help staff cope with psychological sequelae of assaults by patients." *Hospital Community Psychiatry* 42:935-938.

Flannery, R.B., et al. (1994). "Risk Factors for psychiatric inpatient assaults on staff." *Mental Health Administration* 21:24-31.

Flannery, R.B., et al. (1995). "The Assaulted Staff Action Program (ASAP): Guidelines for Fielding a Team." In Vandenbos, G.R. and Bulatao, E.Q. (Eds.). *Violence on the Job* 327-342. Washington, DC: American Psychological Association.

Hales, T., et al. (1988). "Occupational Injuries Due to Violence." *Journal of Occupational and Environmental Medicine* 30(6): 483-487.

Hunter, R.D. (1999). "Convenience Store Robbery Revisited: A Review of Prevention Results." Journal of Security Administration 22(1): pp. 1-14

Hunter, R.D. (1990). "Convenience store robbery in Tallahassee: A Reassessment", FL: Journal of Security Administration.

Hunter, R.D. and Jeffery, C.R. (1991). "Environmental Crime Prevention: An Analysis of Convenience Store Robberies," *Security Journal* 2(2): 78-83.

Jeffery, C.R., Hunter, R.D., and Griswold, J. (1987). "Crime Prevention and Computer Analysis of Convenience Store Robberies in Tallahassee, Florida," *Florida Police Journal* 34: 65-69.

Kinney, J.A., and Johnson, D.L. (1993). *Breaking Point: the Workplace Violence Epidemic and What to Do about It*. Chicago, IL: National Safe Workplace Institute.

Kraus, J.F., Blander, B., and McArthur, D.L. (1995). "Incidence, Risk Factors and Prevention Strategies for Work-related Assault Injuries: A Review of What is Known, What Needs to Be Known, and Countermeasures for Intervention. *Annual Review of Public Health* (16)355-79.

Liberty Mutual (2004). Liberty mutual workplace safety index: the direct costs and leading causes of workplace injuries. Boston, MA: Liberty Mutual, 4 pp. [http://www.libertymutual.com/omapps/ContentServer?cid=1078439448036&pagename=ResearchCenter%2FDocument%2FShowDoc&c=Document].

Matchulat, J.J. (2007). "Separating Fact from Fiction about Workplace Violence." *Employee Relations Law Journal* 33(2) 14-22.

NIOSH (2006). *Workplace Violence Prevention Strategies and Research Needs*. Conference held in Baltimore, Maryland, November 17-19, 2004. Cincinnati, OH: U.S. Department of Health and Human Services, Centers for Disease and Control Prevention, National

Institute for Occupational Safety and Health. DHHS (NIOSH) Publication number 2006-144. [www.cdc.gov/niosh/docs/2006-144]

Northwestern National Life Employee Benefits Division. (1993). *Fear and Violence in the Workplace*. Minneapolis, MN: Northwestern National Life Insurance Company.

Pearson, G.W. (2005). "Controlling the Risk of Violence in the Retail Workplace." *Risk Management*.

Reiss, A.J., Jr., and Roth, J.A. (Eds.). (1993). *Understanding and Preventing Violence*. Washington, DC: National Academy Press.

Rugala, E.A., and Isaacs, A.R. (2004). *Workplace violence: Issues in response*. Quantico, VA: FBI Academy, Federal Bureau of Investigation, National Center for the Analysis of Violent Crime, Critical Incident Response Group [www.fbi.gov/publications/violence.pdf].

Schreiber, B. (1991). "Survey of Convenience Store Crime and Security." Convenience store security: report and recommendations. Alexandria, VA: National Association of Convenience Stores.

Toscano, G. and Weber, W. (1995). Violence in the Workplace. Washington, DC: U.S. Department of Labor, Bureau of Labor Statistics.

Toscano G. and Windau, J. (1994). "The Changing Character of Fatal Work Injuries." *Fatal Workplace Injuries in 1993: A Collection of Data and Analysis* 6-17. Washington, DC: U.S. Department of Labor, Bureau of Labor Statistics.

U.S. Department of Justice. (1994). *Criminal Victimization in the United States*, 1992. Pub. No. NCJ-145 125. Washington, DC.

U.S. Department of Labor, Bureau of Labor Statistics, (1994). Violence in the Workplace Comes Under Closer Scrutiny. Summary 94-10. Washington, DC.

Virginia Crime Prevention Center. (1993). Violent Crimes in Convenience Stores: Analysis of Crimes, Criminals, and Costs. House Document No. 30, Richmond, VA: Commonwealth of Virginia.

Washington Crime News Services. (1994). "New Police Approach Reduces Convenience Store Crime." *Crime Control Digest* 28(1): 1, 4-5.

Workers' Compensation Board of British Columbia. (1995). Take Care: How to Develop and Implement a Workplace Violence Prevention Program (A Guide for Small Business). Vancouver, BC: Workers' Compensation Board of British Columbia.

Zahn, M.A. and Sagi, P.C. (1987). "Stranger Homicides in Nine American Cities." *Journal of Criminal Law & Criminology* 78(2): 377-397.

References

U.S. Department of Justice, Bureau of Justice Statistics. (2001). *National Crime Victimization Survey. Violence in the Workplace*, 1993-99. www.ojp.gov/bjs/pub/pdf/vw99.pdf

U.S. Department of Labor, Bureau of Labor Statistics. (2008). *Census of Fatal Occupational Injuries*, 2006. www.bls.gov/iif/oshwc/cfoi/cftb0215.pdf

U.S. Department of Labor, Bureau of Labor Statistics. (2007). *Survey of Occupational Injuries and Illnesses*, 2006. www.bls.gov/iif/oshwc/osh/case/ostb1796.pdf

U.S. Department of Labor, Bureau of Labor Statistics. (2006). *Survey of Workplace Violence Prevention*, 2005. www.bls.gov/iif/osh_wpvs.htm

OSHA®
Occupational Safety and
Health Administration

OSHA Assistance

OSHA can provide extensive help through a variety of programs, including technical assistance about effective safety and health programs, state plans, workplace consultations, and training and education.

Safety and Health Management System Guidelines

Effective management of worker safety and health protection is a decisive factor in reducing the extent and severity of work-related injuries and illnesses and their related costs. In fact, an effective safety and health management system forms the basis of good worker protection, can save time and money, increase productivity and reduce employee injuries, illnesses and related workers' compensation costs.

To assist employers and workers in developing effective safety and health management systems, OSHA published recommended Safety and Health Program Management Guidelines (54 *Federal Register* (16): 3904-3916, January 26, 1989). These voluntary guidelines can be applied to all places of employment covered by OSHA.

The guidelines identify four general elements critical to the development of a successful safety and health management system:

* Management leadership and worker involvement,
* Worksite analysis,
* Hazard prevention and control, and
* Safety and health training.

The guidelines recommend specific actions, under each of these general elements, to achieve an effective safety and health management system. The *Federal Register* notice is available online at www.osha.gov.

State Programs

The *Occupational Safety and Health Act of 1970* (OSH Act) encourages states to develop and operate their own job safety and health plans. OSHA approves and monitors these plans. Twenty-five states, Puerto Rico and the Virgin Islands currently operate approved state plans: 22 cover both private and public (state and local government) employment; Connecticut, Illinois, New Jersey, New York and the Virgin Islands cover the public sector only. States and territories with their own OSHA-approved occupational safety and health plans must adopt standards identical to, or at least as effective as, the Federal OSHA standards.

Consultation Services

Consultation assistance is available on request to employers who want help in establishing and maintaining a safe and healthful workplace. Largely funded by OSHA, the service is provided at no cost to the employer. Primarily developed for smaller employers with more hazardous operations, the consultation service is delivered by state governments employing professional safety and health consultants. Comprehensive assistance includes an appraisal of all mechanical systems, work practices, and occupational safety and health hazards of the workplace and all aspects of the employer's present job safety and health program. In addition, the service offers assistance to employers in developing and implementing an effective safety and health program. No penalties are proposed or citations issued for hazards identified by the consultant. OSHA provides consultation assistance to the employer with the assurance that his or her name and firm and any information about the workplace will not be routinely reported to OSHA enforcement staff. For more information concerning consultation assistance, see OSHA's website at www.osha.gov.

Strategic Partnership Program

OSHA's Strategic Partnership Program helps encourage, assist and recognize the efforts of partners to eliminate serious workplace hazards and achieve a high level of worker safety and health. Most strategic partnerships seek to have a broad impact by building cooperative relationships with groups of employers and workers. These partnerships are voluntary relationships between OSHA, employers, worker representatives, and others (e.g., trade unions, trade and professional associations, universities, and other government agencies).

For more information on this and other agency programs, contact your nearest OSHA office, or visit OSHA's website at www.osha.gov.

OSHA Training and Education

OSHA area offices offer a variety of information services, such as technical advice, publications, audiovisual aids and speakers for special engagements. OSHA's Training Institute in Arlington Heights, IL, provides basic and advanced courses in safety and health for Federal and state compliance officers, state consultants, Federal agency personnel, and private sector employers, workers and their representatives.

The OSHA Training Institute also has established OSHA Training Institute Education Centers to address the increased demand for its courses from the private sector and from other federal agencies. These centers are colleges, universities, and nonprofit organizations that have been selected after a competition for participation in the program.

OSHA also provides funds to nonprofit organizations, through grants, to conduct workplace training and education in subjects where OSHA believes there is a lack of workplace training. Grants are awarded annually.

For more information on grants, training and education, contact the OSHA Training Institute, Directorate of Training and Education, 2020 South Arlington Heights Road, Arlington Heights, IL 60005, (847) 297-4810, or see Training on OSHA's website at www.osha.gov. For further information on any OSHA program, contact your nearest OSHA regional office listed at the end of this publication.

Information Available Electronically

OSHA has a variety of materials and tools available on its website at www.osha.gov. These include electronic tools, such as *Safety and Health Topics, eTools, Expert Advisors*; regulations, directives and publications; videos and other information for employers and workers. OSHA's software programs and eTools walk you through challenging safety and health issues and common problems to find the best solutions for your workplace.

OSHA Publications

OSHA has an extensive publications program. For a listing of free items, visit OSHA's website at www.osha.gov or contact the OSHA Publications Office, U.S. Department of Labor, 200 Constitution Avenue, NW, N-3101, Washington, DC 20210; telephone (202) 693-1888 or fax to (202) 693-2498.

Contacting OSHA

To report an emergency, file a complaint, or seek OSHA advice, assistance, or products, call (800) 321-OSHA or contact your nearest OSHA Regional or Area office listed at the end of this publication. The teletypewriter (TTY) number is (877) 889-5627.

Written correspondence can be mailed to the nearest OSHA Regional or Area Office listed at the end of this publication or to OSHA's national office at: U.S. Department of Labor, Occupational Safety and Health Administration, 200 Constitution Avenue, N.W., Washington, DC 20210.

By visiting OSHA's website at www.osha.gov, you can also:
- File a complaint online,
- Submit general inquiries about workplace safety and health electronically, and
- Find more information about OSHA and occupational safety and health.

Occupational Safety and
Health Administration

OSHA Regional Offices

Region I
(CT*, ME, MA, NH, RI, VT*)
JFK Federal Building, Room E340
Boston, MA 02203
(617) 565-9860

Region II
(NJ*, NY*, PR*, VI*)
201 Varick Street, Room 670
New York, NY 10014
(212) 337-2378

Region III
(DE, DC, MD*, PA, VA*, WV)
The Curtis Center
170 S. Independence Mall West
Suite 740 West
Philadelphia, PA 19106-3309
(215) 861-4900

Region IV
(AL, FL, GA, KY*, MS, NC*, SC*, TN*)
61 Forsyth Street, SW, Room 6T50
Atlanta, GA 30303
(404) 562-2300

Region V
(IL*, IN*, MI*, MN*, OH, WI)
230 South Dearborn Street
Room 3244
Chicago, IL 60604
(312) 353-2220

Region VI
(AR, LA, NM*, OK, TX)
525 Griffin Street, Room 602
Dallas, TX 75202
(972) 850-4145

Region VII
(IA*, KS, MO, NE)
Two Pershing Square
2300 Main Street, Suite 1010
Kansas City, MO 64108-2416
(816) 283-8745

Region VIII
(CO, MT, ND, SD, UT*, WY*)
1999 Broadway, Suite 1690
PO Box 46550
Denver, CO 80202-5716
(720) 264-6550

Region IX
(AZ*, CA*, HI*, NV*, and American Samoa,
Guam and the Northern Mariana Islands)
90 7th Street, Suite 18-100
San Francisco, CA 94103
(415) 625-2547

Region X
(AK*, ID, OR*, WA*)
1111 Third Avenue, Suite 715
Seattle, WA 98101-3212
(206) 553-5930

* These states and territories operate their own OSHA-approved job safety and health programs and cover state and local government employees as well as private sector employees. The Connecticut, Illinois, New Jersey, New York and Virgin Islands plans cover public employees only. States with approved programs must have standards that are identical to, or at least as effective as, the Federal OSHA standards.

Note: To get contact information for OSHA Area Offices, OSHA-approved State Plans and OSHA Consultation Projects, please visit us online at www.osha.gov or call us at 1-800-321-OSHA.